A NATION
OF NO FEAR
OF GOD

A NATION OF NO FEAR OF GOD

BRUCE ZAVATSKY

XULON PRESS

Xulon Press
2301 Lucien Way #415
Maitland, FL 32751
407.339.4217
www.xulonpress.com

Paperback ISBN-13: 978-1-66284-633-5
Ebook ISBN-13: 978-1-66284-634-2

*This book is dedicated to all of those,
past and present, who lay down their lives
for the sake of the Gospel of Christ.*

Table of Contents

Introduction

The reason for this writing rests in what I see as a primary issue throughout the world. Additionally, I fully see this as a result of man's conscious choice to refuse to accept responsibility, and recognize the reality of accountability.

Throughout this writing, as the Lord directs and leads, I hope to share appropriate definitions and Scripture to show the reader how I reached my conclusions.

At this point, you are probably asking yourself what this sin issue is. Well, I see that the heart of the sin issue is found in Romans 3:18:

> "...there is **no fear of God** before their eyes." (NKJV)

The preceding verse testifies to the condition of the heart, as manifested in the practices of the people spoken of in Romans 1:16-32 and Romans 3:10-18. As you study these texts, you will notice that neither God, nor His word, nor His standard, nor His authority is even considered by these individuals.

As the writing progresses, this will be explained further. Because I not only see this in the secular world, this sin has also become very prominent in the "Christianity" of today. (I put Christianity in quotes for a reason, which will become evident as we continue).

The first chapter of this writing begins with the textual definitions in the use of certain words to grasp the fullest meaning based on God's standard, not man's. It is my prayer that those who read this writing would prayerfully consider the teaching, and honestly evaluate their walk with the Lord. This is something that I am doing as the Lord leads and guides me in this undertaking.

It is interesting to me that our nation, which was founded on the principles of the Bible, now rejects everything but sin. This testifies to the reality that "truth" is not being presented and accepted as relative, but "truth" is compartmentalized. It is the culture (i.e. government) that is teaching people how to think, according to a certain criteria or agenda. I am sorry, this is not education, but indoctrination.

When I say that truth is compartmentalized, I mean that there is often a different "truth" for marriage, sexuality, ministers, laymen, government, people, and lying, or a "truth" for... You can see what I mean. This is why we see young people today using their "Sunday truth" in church, but on Monday they use their "around friends truth" for the rest of the week. No standard is set.

May the Lord be glorified as we respond to His leading and the Holy Spirit's convicting power and presence.

VERITAS

CHAPTER 1

The Definitions

I am starting with the definitions because I fully believe that there is a complete misunderstanding, and a misrepresentation of "fear," as presented in the Scriptures. This is the reason that the culture, the church, and households are in the state that they are in today.

From what I have seen, theologically, there are four main categories of "fear," which can be seen in Scripture, even though the Bible uses numerous other words to denote "fear."

In giving these definitions, and the use of the word, they are certainly not exhaustive, nor are they listed in order of importance. However, I would like the reader to understand that each of us is truly accountable to God, and responsible to Him for how we live and "divide" (i.e. handle) His Word: (See Rom. 14:12; 2 Cor. 5:10; 2 Tim. 2:15; 2 Tim. 4:1)

> "So then each of us (Paul includes himself) shall give account of himself to God." (Rom. 14:12)

For we must all appear before the Judgment seat of Christ, that each one may receive the things done in the body, according to what he has done, whether good or bad." (2 Cor. 5:10)

...rightly dividing the word of truth. (2 Tim. 2:15)

I charge you therefore before God and the Lord Jesus Christ, who will judge the living and the dead at His appearing and His kingdom. (2 Tim. 4:1)

I used these verses solely for the purpose of verifying that everyone, believers included, are still accountable to Christ as seen in Psa. 10:13. Being in Christ is not a license to sin, nor is it excusable for someone who claims Christ, to also violate the standard set forth by God in His Word. These verses are only a small sample of the Scripture which could have been cited here. I hope that you can think of others, which can be used to substantiate this teaching of biblical accountability.

I see each of these verses as a warning from God, preparing us for what we, as believers, can expect and or anticipate.

The first "fear" that I would like to address is "Holy Fear." This fear is a reverential awe of God, which places

God, His Word (since He inspired it), His authority, and His standard far above that of anyone or anything else. This fear is God-given, and it enables and compels the true believer to obey God's Word, and to hate and shun all forms of evil:

> And I will make an everlasting covenant with them, That I will not turn away from doing them good; but I will put My fear in their hearts so that they will not depart from Me. (Jer. 32:40)

> And He said, "Do not lay your hand on the lad, or do anything to him; for now I know that you fear God, since you have not withheld your son, your only son, from Me." (Gen. 22:12)

> Therefore, having these promises, beloved, let us cleanse ourselves from all filthiness of the flesh and spirit, perfecting holiness in the fear of God. (2 Cor. 7:1)

This "fear" is spoken of approximately forty-four times in the New Testament. The Strong's Concordance number is 5401. However, by textual use, we can see "fear" present in different passages.

It is this fear that is the beginning of wisdom:

> The fear of the Lord is the beginning of wisdom; A good understanding have all those who do His commandments. His praise endures forever. (Psa. 111:10)

It is this "fear" that is the core of uprightness:

> The fear of the Lord is to hate evil; Pride and arrogance and the evil way and the perverse mouth I hate. (Prov. 8:13)

It is this "fear" that is the whole duty of man:

> Let us hear the conclusion of the whole matter: Fear God and keep His commandments, for this is man's all. (Eccles. 12:13)

This "fear" is spoken of approximately forty-eight times in the Old Testament. The Strong's Concordance numbers are 3372, 3373, 3374. However, by textual use, we can see this "fear" also spoken of in different passages.

One thing that becomes apparent in these, as well as other passages of Scripture is that true worship of, and obedience to God, is synonymous with this fear of God. Can anyone say that they are truly worshipping God, or even obeying Him, without this "fear" being present?

> Come, you children, Listen to me; I will
> teach you the fear of the Lord. (Psa. 34:11)

> Your own wickedness will correct you, and
> your backslidings will rebuke you. Know
> therefore and see that it is an evil and bitter
> thing that you have forsaken the Lord your
> God, and the fear of Me is not in you," says
> the Lord of hosts. (Jer. 2:19)

> ...a devout man and one who feared God
> with all his household. (Act. 10:2)

> (Read Psa. 34:11-14 to acquire a proper
> understanding.)

For the true believer, there should always be this reverential awe of God before Him, as the majesty and glory of God has never changed. It is this godly fear that stimulates the believer to pursue holiness.

> Therefore, having these promises, beloved,
> let us cleanse ourselves from all filthiness of
> the flesh and spirit, perfecting holiness in
> the fear of God. (2 Cor. 7:1)

I do not know if you realize it or not, but the perfecting of holiness cannot come about if the fear of God is not present.

There is much more that can be written about this "fear," but this should be sufficient to whet your appetite, to dig even deeper into God's Word. I pray that you do honestly evaluate your walk with the Lord, as all of us should do so continuously.

The next "fear" that I would like to address is what Scripture calls the "fear of man." Under this "fear," there are three primary identifiers that we need to be aware of:

1) A true and genuine regard for men, such as masters and magistrates.
2) A blind dread of man and what he is capable of doing to or against us.
3) (This is in a unique sense only) A Christ-like concern for man, lest they be ruined by sin.

Now I would like to examine each of these identifiers to help get a fuller grasp of the impact of "fear."

1) A true genuine regard for men, such as masters and magistrates:

Render therefore to all their due: taxes to whom taxes are due, customs to whom customs, fear to whom fear, honor to whom honor. (Rom. 13:7)

Servants, be submissive to your master with all fear, not only to the good and gentle, but also to the harsh. (1 Pet. 2:18)

In this aspect of the "fear of men," it appears that this is speaking of holding someone in high esteem, with respect.

2) A blind dread of man and what he is capable of doing to or against us:

Only do not rebel against the Lord, nor fear the people of the land, for they are our bread; their protection has departed from them, and the Lord is with us. Do not fear them. (Num. 14:9)

The fear of man brings a snare, but whoever trusts in the Lord shall be safe. (Prov. 29:25)

Do not say, 'a conspiracy,' concerning all that this people call a conspiracy, nor be afraid of their threats, nor be troubled. (Isa. 8:12)

In this aspect of the "fear of men," we see this as being afraid of or intimidated by. When this fear is present, it has almost a paralyzing effect, restricting its victims from being fully effective or useful for the Lord. We see this in Matthew 10:28, and 1 Peter 3:15.

(This is in a unique sense only) A Christian concern for man, lest they be ruined by sin:

> I was with you in weakness, in fear, and in much trembling. (1 Cor. 2:3)

> But I fear, lest somehow, as the serpent deceived Eve by his craftiness, so your minds may be corrupted from the simplicity that is in Christ. (2 Cor. 11:3, NKJV)

In this aspect of the "fear of men," it seems that a more accurate name would be "fear for men." This fear is genuinely manifested toward others, in the life of the true believer, out of a realization of man's sinful condition and or state. It seems to me that the only resolution to this fear is found in 1 John:

> There is no fear in love; but perfect love casts out fear, because fear involves torment. But he who fears has not been made perfect in love. (1 Jn. 4:18)

Only this love of, for, and toward God is able to cast out (i.e. deliver) anyone from this fear. This love generates a perfect peace, as it correctly places one's trust solely in Christ.

> You will keep him in perfect peace, whose mind is stayed on You, because he trusts in You. (Isa. 26:3)

> ... and the peace of God, which surpasses all understanding, will guard your hearts and minds through Christ Jesus.(Phil. 4:7)

Even though fear is not mentioned in either of these verses, it suggests to me (I know that it might be a stretch to think this) that fear cannot exist in "perfect peace." They cannot, and do not exist together.

As stated earlier, there are other words used for fear in Scripture, as well as other definitions. However, I wanted to target these two for a specific reason, as will become evident as this writing continues.

CHAPTER 2

The Tremors of a
Nation in Crisis

A while ago, there was a slogan, of sorts, that has lost
some of its momentum, but still persists today. I saw
it on bumper stickers, T-shirts, TV advertisements, and in
varied presentations throughout the nation. It seemed to be
present at almost every turn.

Additionally, by conduct, it seemed to be embraced
by most people, on every level of our society and or culture, even in the church. I am sure that you know what that
slogan was. It was 'No Fear.'

I fully see that this philosophy is the root cause for the
present condition and state of this nation. Moreover, the
main thrust of this philosophy is the first definition of fear
addressed in Chapter 1. That is the "fear of God," which is
stated in Psalms 36:1 and Romans 3:18: "… there is no fear
of God before their eyes." This is the reason that immorality,
deception, corruption, injustice, and unrighteousness run
rampant on all levels, without any fear of consequence. This
is why churches are afraid to administer church discipline

for the purpose of restoration. This is why laws are not applied to all men equally. This is why truth is subject to interpretation and or opinion, and so on.

Although this context speaks to the nation of Israel, I see that there are striking similarities to the practices of this nation: (I would suggest that the entire chapter be read with this in mind)

> Alas sinful nation, a people laden with iniquity, brood of evildoers, children who are corrupters! They have forsaken the Lord, They provoked to anger the Holy One of Israel, They have turned away backward. (Isa. 1:4)

I like the NKJV in this verse because it speaks of the insulting manner and or fashion of the rebellion of the people of the nation: "... they have turned away backward."

I would like to suggest something about this indictment, which truly fits the context. The people, by practice, knew what the Lord had required of them in obedience. However, they only went through the motions. They lost the focus, meaning, intent, and foundation of the standard that God had set forth. They knew what God had said (in other words, they were facing Him). The context testifies to that. The insulting part comes because they were facing Him when they turned away (i.e. changed or ignored what

He said, to set their own standard, with a flavor of "God" mixed in).

How many times have you told or explained something to someone, instructing them on how to do it and why you want it done the way that you tell them, only to have them acknowledge your instruction, but do the task their own way? Is it not an insult to you to have someone tell you through their actions that they know better than you, even though you are the one that fully understands the ins and outs of the task? I see that the nation of Israel, as well as this nation, and even the church, did -- and are doing this -- to God today.

Let me give some examples of this to emphasize further how far the nation, the world, and even the church has renounced God and demonstrated the "No Fear" approach toward God in our practices.

Is it a coincidence that one of the presidential limousines is called "the Beast?" Why did Barack Obama accept worship as being the "savior" of this nation? (You can Google the pictures of him as being "crucified" in a similar manner to Christ, if you doubt what I am saying). Why would he not deny, reject, or even correct this presentation, instead of rejoicing in it? Why is the inscription on the Euro that of the woman of the book of Revelation, chapter 17? Why are the stars on the flag of the European Union in the form of a circle, and are upside down pentagrams, which is a satanic symbol - calling down the power of Satan? These are just a few of the examples that can be sighted. Nevertheless, is this not enough to cause people to question what is really going on? Is this really just a coincidence?

Let me share something with you at this point, which will be expounded on during this writing. There are more "religious training" institutions (words purposely chosen), "Christian" resources (bookstores, magazines, etc.), "Christian" entertainment (i.e. movies, DVDs, radio, CDs, etc.), and access to "Christian" teaching (social media in various forms). We have the capacity to possess approximately fourteen different translations of the Bible in every household in this nation. Consequently, we are without excuse (See Rom. 1:20). This nation was founded on the principles of God's Word, yet, we continue to go out of our way to provoke God to anger, and invite His judgment. I see this as "turning away backward;" we are facing Him!

Look carefully at this next verse:

> Why should you be stricken again? You will
> revolt more and more. The whole head is
> sick, the whole heart faints. (Isa. 1:5)

Here, the Lord testifies to the nation that they will continue to increase in their sins, on all levels (i.e. from the head to the foot), even though He brings judgment against them. The nation refused to recognize their sinful state, refused to respond to the chastening of the Lord, and refused to learn from the judgments which the Lord was bringing against their sinful practices. Instead of responding to God's correction, they continued to blame God (See Gen. 3).

> From the sole of the foot even to the head,
> there is no soundness in it, but wounds and
> bruises and putrefying sores; They have not
> been closed or bound up, or soothed with
> ointment. (Isa. 1:6)

There was nowhere that the sins of the nation were not present (See Isa. 24:2; Hos. 4:9), and there was nothing being done about it. This is why God testifies to the nation that their sins are like wounds that are left untreated. Wounds that are left untreated eventually become incurable.

When you continue to read and study Isaiah, you will find that God told the nation what they could expect if they continued in their sinful practices. He also tells them what their "obedience" is like to Him (See Isa. 1:11). Nevertheless, in His love, grace, mercy, and care, He also gives them the resolution (See Isa. 1:9, 18-20). He has done this for this nation as well. However, are we, like the nation of Israel, not paying attention? What will God have to do before we wake up?

I believe that this nation is truly following in the same rebellious path as the nation of Israel has for so long, only we are doing it on a grander scale. Tell me: if this nation does have a genuine, biblical "fear of God," would it, or the church, be in the state or condition that it is in now? Can each of us honestly, biblically evaluate our lives and truly say we are part of the resolution (i.e. restoring a biblical fear of God?) Alternatively, upon evaluation, will we find that we are a part of the problem (i.e. fearing man?)

I fully believe that the "fear of God," as defined earlier, must be recognized, understood, embraced, and lived out, for this, or any other nation, to know God's blessings to the fullest. **We need to repent!**

For further clarification, I do not use the term "God" in a generic fashion. This is not *a* "god" or any "god" to which I refer, but to *the* God: The God of Abraham, Isaac, and Jacob. The Holy One of Israel. The One who was, and is, and who is to come, the Almighty. The "I AM." The Lord Jesus Christ. The God of the Bible. This is the God that we need to fear, not the one who is conjured up and promoted by the imagination of man. I want to close this chapter with this thought: why did God bring judgment upon the earth back in Genesis 6 and 7? Was it not because the imagination and intention of the thoughts of man's heart "was evil continually?"

Therefore, any god who is not the God of the Bible, would have to come from the imagination of man's heart. Since God defined the imagination of man's heart as evil continually, then would that not make any god that came from that continually evil imagination, continually evil also? If that kind of god was served, worshipped, and promoted anywhere, should not those who do so also expect judgment from the true God?

The only way that God's judgment will not come is if God or His standard has changed (See Mal. 3:6; Heb. 13:8). All we have to do is look around to see the supernatural expression of God's displeasure to see that neither He, nor His standard, has changed. I believe that what we see today is God's wake up call for the nations. The problem is that people are not paying attention, and even if they do show any kind of response, they hit the "snooze bar" and go back to sleep. The ultimate question is: what time is it for this nation?

CHAPTER 3

Examine the Evidence

I would like to start this chapter with a particular verse from Romans 1:

> ... who, knowing the righteous judgment of God, that those who practice such things, are deserving of death, not only do the same but also approve of those who practice them. (Rom. 1:32)

(We would all do well to read verses 18-31 now).

According to God's standard, you do not have to just practice the sins mentioned in verses 18-31 to invite, or be the recipients of, God's judgment, but even the approval of the practices, and those who practice them will do that (See Psa. 50:16-23; Hos. 7:3).

"approve" – officially accepting as satisfactory; believe that someone or something is good and acceptable.

(Definition is from Oxford English Dictionary and Strong's # - 4909)[1]

You may be asking why I would start this chapter with this verse. I think that the reason will become clear as this writing continues.

I have seen and heard "Christians" and non-Christians alike, living their lives contrary to even the basic principles of Scripture. In addition, the problem comes because there is no remorse, repentance, or regret. The majority of these people justify their actions, twist the Scriptures to suit their own purposes, or go back to the root history of mankind (See Gen. 3). When confronted by God (or His Word), it was someone else's fault, even to the point of blaming God when judgment came. How many of us really accept or embrace rebuke and or correction? Isn't that why God gave us His Word (See 2 Tim. 3:16-17)? If someone corrects us biblically (according to the whole counsel of God), are we willing to hear and allow the Lord to make the necessary changes in our lives?

> Then the man said, "The woman who You gave me ...she gave me..." And the Lord God said to the woman, "What is this you have done? And the woman said, "The serpent deceived me." (Gen. 3:12-13)

Is this a common problem today? How many times have we heard or seen people abuse or misuse God's Word for their own personal gain (i.e. "The Lord told me ...," or "The Lord showed me...," or "I prayed about it and the Lord led me to ...")? These people "prayed" about something; they felt a "peace" about it, and many times, it has led them to an action or teaching that is contrary to even the plainest meaning of God's Word. When you question them about it, using God's Word in its context, do they still defend their position? Do they use God's Word as it is written, or do they read something into it for the purpose of justifying their position? Has your view become antiquated, or old-fashioned Christianity ("That was written for them back then;" "This is a new age;" "The Bible needs to be updated to accommodate the way we think and do things today")? Do any of these sound familiar, or similar to any argument that you have heard?

Let us look back at the example of Adam and Eve. Both Adam and Eve were standing right there, in God's presence. He did not utter dark sayings; He spoke very plainly to them (See John 10 and 11). Satan came to them in a different voice and tempted them with words that were contrary to the plain, direct words of God. He tempted Adam and Eve to doubt the plain meaning and intention of God's Word. I guess my question would be, if you (Adam and Eve) talked with God directly, how could there be any misinterpretation, misunderstanding, or deception, let alone blaming God for any judgments that transpired because of disobedience? Would this not include this nation today? As stated before, how is it that we are questioning or blaming God for the state of this nation? Did we not do this to ourselves?

Both "Christians" and non-Christians alike are equally as guilty, as far as I can see. Obviously, like Adam and Eve, we seek something other than God's glory and standard.

We will be looking at other passages of Scripture in this chapter, but I wanted to start with these two:

> I will worship toward Your Holy temple and praise Your name. For Your loving-kindness and Your truth; For You have magnified Your word above all Your name. (Psa. 138:2)

> (See also John 17:17).

In this verse, we see that God Himself puts a value on His Word that is even above that of His own name. So, if God Himself has done this, should not we value His Word in that same fashion?

> We also have the prophetic word made more sure, which we do well to heed as a light that shines in a dark place, until the day dawns and the morning star arises in your hearts; knowing this first, that no prophecy of Scripture is of any private interpretation, for prophecy never came by

the will of man, but holy men of God spoke
as they were moved by the Holy Spirit. (2
Pet. 1:19-21)

According to this passage of Scripture, God's Word and standard are not to be changed for any reason. God gave it the way it is, and it is to be taught, accepted, and lived out before men, just as it is written, with no deviations. We do not have the right, privilege, or authority to interpret His Word any way we choose. Obviously, there are many other Bible verses that could be cited here to support this teaching (See Deut. 4:2; 1 Kings 22:13-14; Matt. 28:19-20; 2 Tim. 2:15-16, 3:16-17; Rev. 22:18-19). However, I think that these are sufficient to get to the point.

Therefore, it does not matter if you have a "peace" about something that you have committed to prayer. If your decision violates the plain meaning of God's Word in any respect, what kind of "peace" is it and where did it come from? The ultimate question is, can anyone really say, and believe, that they have the true "fear of God" if they live contrary to the Word which He has inspired and valued above His own name?

I would like to look at a couple of other verses, and discuss some examples and or events which manifest the transition of this nation from its foundation (i.e. fear of God), to its deteriorated state that we see today (i.e. fear of man).

> And the Lord said to Moses, 'Go, get down!
> For your people who brought out of the
> land of Egypt have corrupted themselves.
> (Exod. 32:7)

Please notice how the Lord describes the people to whom He granted freedom: "self-corrupted." The blame is clearly placed at the feet of the people. They made the choice to be "stiff-necked." God uses this term on six different occasions to describe His people. This was because they willingly refused to accept the authority of God and His Word to govern them. Their entire approach to God, and perspective of Him, was completely changed from previously (see Exod. 20) when they saw and knew the power and presence of God in the nation. Does this sound familiar?

> You shall not at all do as we are doing here,
> every man doing whatever is right in his
> own eyes. (Deut. 12:8)

Notice, it is that standard of man that had replaced God and His standard in the hearts and lives of the people of the nation. Does this also sound familiar? It saddens me to say that this is also going on in the churches of today. I have seen this in several different aspects of Christianity today. Christians today are not being equipped to be Bereans (See Acts 17:11), but are being programmed to think the way a church, denomination, or teacher wants them to think. Want proof of this? The next time you hear something taught from a pulpit, in a classroom, or at a Bible conference that is contrary to the Word of God, question it. You should anyway; just because that person in front of the crowd or congregation has a degree does not mean that they are always correct. It is the same for this writing. If there is anything shared that is a blatant contradiction to Scripture, then challenge it. However, do it according to the standard that God has set forth, not by your own standard, and always in love, with meekness and fear.

> In those days there was no king in Israel;
> everyone did what was right in his own
> eyes. (Judg. 21:25)

(As a side note: since we did not have an "election" according to legal or godly standards, we also have no leadership in the country).

Nevertheless, putting that aside for now, everyone is still doing what is right in his own eyes. Look at the consequences spoken of by God in Proverbs 14:12, and 16:25. These choices lead only to death.

Let us return to Judges 21:25. Did this nation not have the necessary spiritual leadership at this time as well, even though they did not have a king? Were not the judges also supposed to lead and govern the people in the way of righteousness, according to the standard of God? In addition, if you look back at Judges 2, it only took one generation for this to take hold in the nation. It has been said that, "what one generation accepts as being true, the next generation embraces as being fact." As a reminder at this point, please go back and read Isaiah1, to substantiate that this corruption and or sinful condition had permeated all levels of the nation (i.e. head to the foot).

> You have wearied the Lord with your words Yet you say, 'In what way have we wearied Him?' In that you say, "Everyone who does evil is good in the sight of the Lord, and He delights in them.'" Or, "Where is the God of justice? (Mal. 2:17)

Both of these approaches are an affront and challenge to the authority of God and His Word in the lives of men everywhere. All of these unjust, unrighteous practices, as given in their context, are a result of, "no fear of God before their eyes," and stand as a testimony of the fear of man.

Again, there are many other passages, which can be cited here, but these should be enough to get all of us to dig further into the Word of God. Other passages that could be considered would be Jeremiah 5, 44:15ff; John 9:13ff; and Philippians 2:19-21. This definitely is not exhaustive, but sufficient evidence from God's Word to substantiate the above teaching.

I said that I was going to give examples for this in our nation, and I cannot find a better example than one of the most blatant and recent. That is, as stated earlier, the supposed "election" of the current "administration." Voter fraud, tampering, and deception on varying levels was shown and testified to before the American people on television, radio, social media, and newspapers, etc. The evidence was there for everyone to see. Yet, Biden and Harris assume the role of President and Vice-president. How and why? With this in mind, I want to ask several questions. In all of this, I would like the reader to re-read the first verses, which started this chapter.

Here are the questions:

If Biden and Harris both know that there was fraud, tampering, etc., can either of them claim to be genuine, biblical Christians? (See Prov. 21:6).

If fraud was indeed shown, could a Bible believing Christian maintain that position and remain holy in God's sight? (See 1 Pet. 1:13ff).

In retaining those positions under these suspicious conditions, how does that reflect the "fear of God" (understanding that all of us will give an account to Him)?

If there is intimidation of any sort, on any level, could the person being threatened or intimidated actually claim Christ as their own? Can they honestly claim Christ as their own if their fear of man overshadows their fear of God and their responsibility to others?

How about those who were involved in the "election fraud," the "cover–ups," etc., if there were any (those who took care of the ballots, voting machines, etc.)? If there was any wrongdoing, what was your part, and how much was your integrity worth? Alternatively, does it even matter?

How about the judges who twisted, distorted, or even rejected the evidence that was presented? Will you be declared innocent or guilty when you stand before the Judge of all judges, Presidents, Vice-presidents, congressmen, etc.? (Remember that the Bible, the book by which all men will be judged, in John12:48, gives the proper domain of confession. That domain of confession is: If you have sinned publically, you must also make a public confession. Doing a "behind-the-scenes" confession is not biblical since your sin is public). If you were involved in any dishonest act that affected others, you must tell them and ask for their forgiveness. What will the verdict be? (See Rev. 20:11-14, 21:8). I would suggest that you read these passages very carefully!

Are the decisions and practices of this current "administration" based on the fear of the God of Scripture who is ready to judge the living and the dead? On the other hand, are they based on the promotion of the fear of man? (Based on an honest evaluation of the evidence that has been set before this nation). Everyone needs to remember that all will be revealed in the end, as "the day will declare it."

There are many other questions which could be asked, and of different entities. Still, I think that these are sufficient to cause the reader to arrive at a proper conclusion, based on a biblical evaluation of the current situation.

As a side concern, I do have one primary question for the news media: Is your reporting based on fact, and designed to inform (i.e. the fear of God)? Or rather, is it "tailor made" and slanted to a particular agenda and or objective other than truth (i.e. the fear of man)? Remember that God knows the truth, and He will evaluate each work according to His standard in the Day of Judgment. Are you ready?

I know that many by this point are saying or thinking, "I don't have anything to worry about. I don't believe in God or His Word!" Just one word of warning before the conclusion:

> The fool has said in his heart, "There is no God..." (Psa. 14:1)

> ...do not be deceived, God is not mocked. (Gal. 6:7)

God's existence never has, and never will, depend on whether or not anyone trusts or believes in Him. His existence is shown and proven to us on a daily basis through what we can see.

In the closing of this chapter, there are several verses that I find very pertinent to the sin issues written about here:

> Everyone who is proud in heart is an abomination to the Lord; though they join forces, none will go unpunished. (Prov. 16:5)

(See also Prov. 11:16-21).

The Lord is very concise in His declaration, which coincides with the principle of the verse that started this chapter.

> I will give children to be their princes, And babes shall rule over them. (Isa. 3:4)

> As for My people, children are their oppressors, and women rule over them. O My people! Those who lead you cause you to err, And destroy the way of your path. (Isa. 3:12)

This was written to the nation of Israel, but make no mistake about it. God's judgment will not be withheld from all nations that continue in their sins. For proof of this, read Jeremiah 5 and look at how many times the phrase, "such a nation as this," is used. According to God's warning for the nation, part of His judgment for any sinful nation is that they would have leaders that are incapable of making proper decisions, lack leadership qualities, "get their own way," by whatever means necessary (i.e. children; babes). In addition, women would rule over them. That is not God's blessing on the nation, it was a part of His judgment against the nation (look back at Gen. 3 – as well as other passages). Moreover, those leaders, whom the people put into power, would lead the nation into error, and destroy the hope of the people. They would promote and draw people into a relationship that caused the people to directly or indirectly depend upon them. Keep reading the entire chapters of Isaiah 3 and 5. Do you see any similarities between the practices of Israel, which provoked God to judgment, and the practices of this nation today? If you have not seen the similarities, please read both chapters again. How did God respond to the practices of the nation? I know that I have stated this before, but we really need to grab hold of this.

> "Shall I punish them for these things?" says the Lord. "And shall I not avenge Myself on such a nation as this?" (Jer. 5:9)
>
> (See also Jer. 5:29).

Reading the entire chapter of Jeremiah 5 will help us to understand what invites God's judgment upon any nation. There are approximately thirteen sinful practices mentioned in this chapter, which testifies to how far the nation had chosen to turn away from the Lord, His authority, and His word.

Just a couple of examples to convey what I am talking about:

> "...If there is anyone who executes judgements, Who seeks the truth... (Jer. 5:1)

(There is a lack of justice, and there is a desire for the truth).

> They have lied about the Lord, and said,
> "*It is* not He. Neither will evil come upon
> us, nor shall we see sword or famine. And
> the prophets become wind, for the word *is*
> not in them. Thus shall it be done to them."
> (Jer. 5:12-13)

(There is a false concept of the Lord and His righteous judgments).

How many times have we heard these false prophets of iniquity share these prophecies and projections that never happen? This is not only for the church, but how many times have we heard bogus campaign promises or false projections from the government? Those who are in the church and practice this abuse the name of Christ and the authority of His word. Yet, people still fear them, support them, and follow them. Why? (See Deut. 13:1-5; 18:21-22).

One last thought before closing this chapter: How much of what we as a nation are being told is actually true? How do we know? What is the source of the verification? Has our government and or leadership ever created or used a crisis for its own purpose(s)? (Before you answer that, do some research). Is that not what we see going on today? Is their purpose to develop a deeper dependence or trust in them? Could it possibly be that through fear and or intimidation (i.e. possibly inflated pandemic numbers, false reports, etc.), they are brainwashing people as to what to think and how? If that is not their agenda, why not tell the people the truth and allow them the opportunity to draw proper conclusions, based on the facts? Is that not what teaching, informing, and educating people is all about? Has this nation also become like the people of the nation of Israel in Jeremiah 5:31: "...and My people love to have it so ...". However, do not stop there. Look carefully at God's response to the people in the last part of the verse: "... But what will you do in the end?"

There is much more that can be shared about this subject, but no man can do more, or a better job, than God has already done in His Word. We need to get back to the foundation of Christ and His Word, as it is written. This is the only way that anyone can honestly say that we genuinely fear God, rather than man.

If there is one truth that stands out among the rest, it is this: any nation that does not have or exercise the fear of God, as defined by His Word, that nation cannot hire enough police officers. Our rights and freedoms come from God and can only be retained when that fear of God is maintained. He can and will remove those rights and freedoms when we relinquish, by conscious choice, His proper place in our lives (See Rom. 1:16-32:"...He turned them over..."). How much more proof do we need?

CHAPTER 4

Dark Horse Rising

There is an agenda that is now gaining more momentum every day. It is the agenda of a "New World Order," or a "One World Government." Additionally, the reason that I see this rapid progression is because the people have become willingly ignorant. The fear of God has been purposely replaced by the fear of man, and the people in "leadership roles" are capitalizing on it like a shark that smells blood. The ultimate question in relationship to this is, do we really have proper representation in Washington? Are those people who we have voted for really the voice of the people? Are there more rhinos in power than we know?

In the Bible texts that I shared with you in this writing, the sinful practices that are spoken of are a reflection of the condition of the heart of the people of the nation. And, unfortunately, these sinful practices continue to increase as the fear of God vanishes from our culture. We are becoming more and more culture-oriented than God-fearing. Nonetheless, the Word of God told us that these days would come:

But know this, that in the last days perilous times would come: (2 Tim. 3:1)

But evil men and impostors will grow worse and worse, deceiving and being deceived. (2 Tim. 3:13)

In the days before the Lord's return, the situations, circumstances, events, and people that surround us every day will increasingly get worse. With each "crisis" increasing, do we see the "leaders" stepping in and saying, "Do not worry. Everything is going well. Things are looking up. Trust us, we will take care of everything,"? Do these, or similar words, sound familiar to anyone? Are they not telling the people that they are the answer to the crisis that they have created? Is this not a circular situation? Does this not mandate that they are in complete control and that we do not have the right (given by God) to question them?

Let me ask you a couple of questions. If control and manipulation is not their agenda or purpose, what happens if anyone questions or challenges them? What happens to those who oppose, stand against, disagree with, interfere with, or speak against the government? I am not talking about violent protests of any sort. (That is a topic for another time. I would suggest that the violent protesters read John 18:36. There is more to it than I have time to explain in this writing).

Who is holding them accountable, and how, if no one is allowed to challenge or question them? If there is a grievance against them, to whom do you take it ? (Think about the history of this nation. There were documents and laws established in this nation that forbade absolute power for one individual, unless there was a genuine emergency. Still, it was not up to the one individual to decide what the emergency was or what constituted an emergency).

Is there really justice in our land, as defined by the true Judge in His Word? Is the standard of God upheld? If judges, attorneys, police, etc. abuse or misuse their authority, can we truly say that there is justice in our land? According to founding documents (i.e. The Constitution, Declaration of Independence, etc.) our rights and freedoms come from God. If they come from God, then how can any man, no matter who he is, think that he alone has the authority to revoke those rights, unless he thinks that he is greater than the God who gave those rights? Does anyone else see a problem here? Is this not the fear of man overshadowing and or replacing the fear of God? However, I do realize one primary issue with regard to this, which I touched on previously. I see this as God's response to this nation, which has very little, if any, regard for Him. I can clearly see that God is doing exactly what He said that He would do: He is giving us over to our own sinful desires, passions, and pursuits. His Word teaches that we get the leadership that we deserve.

I chose the title of this chapter based on two particular passages of Scripture; the first is:

> "When He opened the third seal, I heard the third living creature say, 'Come and see.' And I looked and behold a black horse, and he who sat on it had a pair of scales in his hand. And I heard a voice in the midst of the four living creatures saying, 'A quart of wheat for a denarius, and three quarts of barley for a denarius; and do not harm the oil and the wine.'" (Rev. 6:5-6)

These verses in Revelation speak of a literal famine that is yet to come. This famine is the third seal of seven. It will affect the entire world, and a "black horse" represents it. (Stay with me).

The next verses that I would like to look at are:

> "Behold the days are coming," says the Lord GOD "That I will send a famine on the land, Not a famine of bread, Nor a thirst for water, But of hearing the words of the Lord. They shall wander from sea to sea, and from north to east; They shall run to and fro, seeking the word of the Lord, But shall not find it." (Amos 8:11-12)

As stated in these verses, this spiritual famine would blanket the nation, also reminiscent of:

> Help Lord, the godly man ceases! For the faithful disappear from among the sons of men. They speak idly everyone with his neighbor: with flattering lips and a double heart they speak. (Psa. 12:1-2)

The point that I want to make is that this spiritual famine (i.e. "black horse") is continuing to grow in this nation.

Have you ever taken notice of the words and or speeches of our political leaders? How many of them have said what they mean, and mean what they say? How about the bills and or laws that they pass? Are they straight-forward in the writing of these bills and or laws, or are there "piggy-backed" hidden agendas? How about the sermons and or teachings of the "spiritual leaders" of this nation? Some of them have big smiles, their words sound so nice, they tell us that everything is going to be OK, etc. Nevertheless, their message is void of biblical content and authority. Most of the time, their message is based on nothing more than feeling or emotion.

They do not speak the truth. They speak whatever is necessary to draw the hearers into their tangled web of deception. Moreover, the reason so many people are being deceived is that there is no fear of God before their eyes. If there were a genuine fear of God, would there not be an accountability of biblical standard toward these leaders? Are they not flattering people to gain advantage (See Jude 16)? Are they not drawing followers (i.e. disciples) after their own selves (See Acts 20:30)? Are the hearers of the Word not commanded to check out what is being taught, and to challenge the teachers of those things that are contrary to sound doctrine (See Acts 17:11; Rom. 16:17-20; 1 John 4:1-6)?

The only hope that this nation has, or the people of this nation have, is to cry unto the Christ of the Bible, confessing our sins to Him before it is too late (if it is not already), and forsaking those practices which His Word states are sinful (See Prov. 28:13; James 1:22; 1 John 1:8-10). Still, it is the standard of God that must be used to make a proper evaluation, not man's (See Isa. 55:6-11). Anything less has no value or significance (See Isa. 1-2).

CHAPTER 5

A Closer Look

In this chapter, I would like to look at four specific Scripture passages in some detail. With each verse and or passage, I want to ask some questions that I believe, upon honest evaluation, will help each of us to draw a proper conclusion. The questions for each passage will be very similar and therefore may become tedious, boring, or even redundant. Nevertheless, I would ask you to continue on to the end, or even ask some of your own questions in connection with the subject matter of this writing.

> "And I will come near you for judgment:
> I will be a swift witness against sorcerers,
> against adulterers, against perjurers, against
> those who exploit wage earners and widows
> and the fatherless, and against those who
> turn away an alien – because they do not
> fear Me." Says the Lord of hosts. (Mal. 3:5)

We can be very sure that before I start asking the questions, I think I need to provide some definitions so that a fuller understanding of the text can be gleaned.

#1 Sorcerers - One of a Median caste, a magician; a wizard, sorcerer, a pretender to magical powers, a professor to the arts of witchcraft.

(Although not part of the definition, this would include séances, tarot cards, necromancy, psychic readings, and the like). (Strong's #3784)

(Definition is from Vine's Complete Expository Dictionary, Pg. 587)[2].

#2 Pharmakos – an adjective signifying "devoted to magical arts," is used as a noun, "a sorcerer," especially one who uses drugs, potions, spells, enchantments. (Although not a part of this Vine's definition, there is a similar word used in Rev. 21:8; and 22:15. The word used in both Revelation verses is "pharmakia," from where we get our word "pharmaceuticals." This identifies misuse or abuse of drugs and other any controlling substances. I believe that the entirety of the definition of the word is in view based on this text, as well as others).

"Adulterers" – There is a complete misunderstanding about what "adultery" really is. Adultery, as defined by Scripture, includes sexual sins of all kinds, including fornication, sodomy, homosexuality, pornography, and the like.

The reason that it includes or encompasses all sexual sins is because the act of adultery is actually the violation of a covenant. This is why Matt. 5:27- 32 testifies to "just looking with lust" as committing adultery. This is also why adultery is identified in Scripture on two different plains–physical and spiritual (See James 4:4 and Ezek. 16:15ff, 23:43).

"Perjurers"- Those who take and or make a false oath. Those who swear falsely by the name of the Lord. (See Lev. 19:12; Jer. 5:2 and 7, 7:9; Zech. 5:4; and James 5:12).

(Definition from Vine's Complete Expository Dictionary, page 253, Strong's number 7650).[3]

"Those who exploit ..." – To exploit is to abuse, oppress, defraud, or afflict. (See Exod. 22:22-24; Lev. 19:13; Deut. 24:14; Mic. 2:2; Mal. 2:14; James 5:4).

This particular portion of Scripture is for all levels, not just a select few. This includes government agencies: presidents, vice presidents, corporations, bosses, husbands, fathers, etc. Please read the contexts of the verses listed above.

"Those who turn away an alien" -This is a reference to the perversion of justice toward strangers; To deprive the foreigners in the land of justice; exhibition of partiality for or against a foreigner.

(See Exod. 2:18ff; Lev. 19:33; Deut. 10:17ff, 24:17-18, 27:19; Jer. 7:6; Ezek. 27:7ff).

With these definitions and characteristic identifiers in mind, let us ask some pertinent questions. These questions will be based on context, and the provided definitions. (Hint: God has already provided the answer in Malachi 3:5).

One other thought before the questions. Look at the first two sentences of Malachi 3:5. The Lord was not only going to execute judgment against the nation for these practices, but He would also be a "swift witness" against them. This means that since He had full knowledge of their sin, He would bring evidence and testimony (i.e. testify) against them.

Now the questions: (All questions will be based on the understanding of the definitions that were presented above).

Can anyone who practices any form of sorcery honestly say that they have a biblical fear of God? (This would include Wicca, witchcraft, tarot cards, séances, Ouija boards, magic 8 balls, etc. These are not just games, but are actually an introduction into the occult).

Can anyone who is under the influence of a controlling substance actually believe that they have a fear of God (See Eph. 5:15-18)? (This includes, but is not limited to, marijuana, meth, cocaine, any narcotics, etc.)

If there is a dependence on anyone or anything other than God Himself, can we honestly say we fear God?

Can anyone who violates the marriage covenant fully testify to those who are around them that the fear of God dwells within their heart? (See Matt. 19:1-10).

Would not the, "It's OK to look, as long as I don't touch," approach also testify to the lack of the fear of God? (This would include viewing pornographic material of any kind, regardless of how man defines it).

As far as abusing children goes, can anyone actually think that this perversion is a way to demonstrate fear of God? (See Matt. 18:1-9).

When laws are passed that justify the acts of the ungodly, and condemn the just, is the fear of God present or just assumed?

Do the practices of sodomy, homosexuality, child molestation, or any other sexual immorality declare the fear of God in any way? (See Gen. 1 and 2; 1 Cor. 5:9-11, 6:9-11; Gal. 5:16ff; and Rev. 21:8)

How many times have you heard someone take an oath, yet he or she deliberately declares lies?

How about those who declare fallacy, falsehood or lies in Jesus name? (See Jer. 5:2).

How many political leaders, judicial leaders, etc. have taken an oath to protect and serve the people of this nation, yet they continue to abuse their authority and oppress the people who are under their administration? (See Isa. 3:13ff).

How about those who own companies, or run companies for someone else? Do you treat your employees, or those who are under your authority, as Jesus would? Do you overwork some while others are left to do very little? Have you made commitments to them and not followed through? (See Psa. 15).

Are those under your authority treated fairly and equally, or do you show favoritism toward some while abusing others? (See Prov. 28:21) (Do you justify, or make excuses, for the ones that do not do as much as the others?)

How about those who neglect or take advantage of widows and orphans through "government programs," schemes, or laws that benefit only the law-makers and make slaves of the recipients? (I am sure that you can think of some examples, and I am equally sure that you will not have to think too hard).

When you look back at the history of this country and you see how many people who legally entered this country were treated, can this nation honestly say that the fear of God is what generated that treatment? How about today?

Are we now, as a nation, showing partiality toward the "aliens" in our nation and neglecting those who were born here? Is not this forsaking the fear of God, and replacing it with the fear of man? (See Jer. 5:14ff–by principle application).

There are many other questions that I could ask about each of these sinful practices of the nation, but these should suffice in order to cause us to think about our own understanding of these practices.

If the Lord has spoken to your heart, and there are areas of your life that you need to give to Him, please do so before time runs out (See Prov. 28:13).

There is a judgment coming. His judgment and justice will not sleep, nor will it keep silent forever.

> He will not always strive with us, nor will
> He keep His anger forever. He has not
> dealt with us according to our sins, nor
> punished us according to our iniquities.
> (Psa. 103:9-10)

Because I have called and you refused, I have stretched out my hand and no one regarded, Because you disdained all my counsel, and would have none of my reproof, I also will laugh at your calamity; I will mock when your terror comes, When your terror comes like a storm, and your destruction comes like a whirlwind, when distress and anguish come upon you.(Prov. 1:24-27) (Read all of Prov. 1)

But there were also false prophets among the people, even as there will be false teachers among you, who will secretly bring in destructive heresies, even denying the Lord who bought them, and bring on themselves swift destruction. And many will follow their destructive ways, because of whom the way of truth will be blasphemed. By covetousness they will exploit you with deceptive words; for a long time their judgment has been idle, and their destruction does not slumber. (2 Pet. 2:1-3)

I know that there are other parts of Scripture which can be cited here, but I see that these are sufficient for the moment.

The next portion of Scripture that I would like to examine is Romans 1:16-32. Because of the length of this text, I will not write it out in its entirety, but will highlight portions, and hope that you will read it as I ask the following questions. The questions are not exhaustive, but are designed to encourage honest evaluation by the reader about the condition of this nation, the church, and the people of the nation.

Can anyone say that the fear of God is present in his or her lives if there exists a shame for the true Gospel of Christ?

If the gospel (See Isa. 53; John 3:16; I Cor. 15:3ff) is not preached, is the fear of God present?

Can those who suppress the truth (See John 17:17) in unrighteousness claim a reverence for God, knowing that He places the value of His word above His own name?

Can anyone deny creation and hold that they fear the Creator?

Can anyone change the glory of the incorruptible God into that which is corruptible, and still maintain a reverence for God at all?

Can anyone practice idolatry, as described in the text, and identify with any aspect of a biblical fear of God?

How about those who exchange the truth of God for the lie. Where is the fear of God in that practice? Would that not declare God as the liar? (See Rom. 3:4).

Can anyone honestly say that they fear God if they lie, steal, cheat, covet, etc.? (As stated in the context).

Can anyone who agrees with, supports, excuses, or justifies these practices (See Rom. 3:32), even identify with the biblical fear of God? (Even if the government legalizes or condones these practices).

The Lord has already testified against these and other practices based on His standard (His Word). He has also testified against those who would agree with the practices and those who practice them (See Romans 2-3). In doing so, is He not also testifying that the fear of God is not present in the lives of those who agree with, and practice such things?

The next text that I would like to examine is Isaiah 5. Even though the text is written to Israel, all nations can learn from every text in the Bible (See Rom. 15:4). If God judged Israel for these sins, what makes anyone think that God will not judge them for doing the same?

Again, because of the length of the text and limited space, I will not write out the text. I will be issuing challenge questions based on certain points in the text. (Read the 7 "woes" very carefully).

Since the nation was established by God, was founded on the principles of His Word, and He has blessed this nation beyond measure, where is His honor in this nation today?

Why do we go out of our way to do everything we can to provoke Him to anger and judgment?

Instead of being or becoming the people God desires us to be, why do we fight and devour one another?

Can we not see greed is everywhere in this nation? Is anyone honestly content, or do we see or hear of people always wanting more?

Is not drunkenness a major problem in this nation? Do we not see people looking for excuses for alcohol consumption? (See Matt. 24:37-39).

Are people seeking to know or gain understanding about what is going on? On the other hand, do they prefer to be "willingly ignorant?" (More about this later).

How about those who would parade their sins before others without shame?

What about those who challenge or taunt God with regard to His judgment? (See Isa. 5:18-19). Is this really the fear of God as defined by His Word?

Can someone call "good" what God has said is "evil," or call "evil" what God has declared is "good," and still say, "I fear God?" Does this not set the standard of man above the standard established and proven by God? Would this also make God out to be a liar?

What is the standard that we use to determine "good" and "evil," "light" and "dark," "bitter" and "sweet," since it is not the standard of God that we choose to recognize, apply, or accept?

Please read all of Isaiah 5 to see what the Lord's response is, or will be, toward any people or nation who practice, or approve of, those who practice such things.

If you will, come along with me for one more journey. I would like to look at one more passage. I know that may have exhausted your patience by now, so I will not do the same with this passage as with the others. The verses that I want to use here are a bit different from those previously cited.

> All Scripture is given by inspiration of God, and is profitable for doctrine, for reproof, for correction, for instruction in righteousness, that the man of God may be complete, thoroughly equipped for every good work. (2 Tim. 3:16-17)

If the Scriptures are "of God, which they are, and God has told us the purpose for which He gave them to accomplish what He set them forth to do (See Isa. 55:11), why are they not used this way by everyone who names His name?

Is it possible that churches, pastors, teachers, chaplains, etc., fear man, more then they fear God? As I recall, Jesus was not very popular when He was here. Neither were any of His disciples when they shared Him and His word with those around them. In fact, I think I remember reading somewhere that if we do the same, we also will suffer as He did. (See John 15:20; 2 Tim. 3:12).

If God gives Scripture for profit in the four stated areas, and to ultimately equip the man of God for every good work, then what is the man of God being equipped with, when Scripture is twisted, distorted, or misused? (See 2 Tim. 2:15-16; 2 Pet. 3:14-18; Jude 3).

At this point, please look back at the practices that are described prior to verses 16-17 of our context, and then ask this question: In all of this, where is the fear of God?

Do verses 16-17 not testify to the reader that His word was given and or inspired to identify these practices as sin, and to correct thinking and the actions pertaining to these sins, according to His standard? (See Isa. 55:8-11).

In bringing this chapter to a close, my prayer is that the Scriptures that have been shared will cause each one of us to prayerfully, biblically evaluate our relationship with the Lord, and with one another (See Matt. 22:37-40; 2 Cor. 13:4-10).

Prayer:

Lord, help all of us to recognize all of the areas in our own lives where we have violated Your Word: The places where we have given ourselves over to the fear of man, rather than standing firm in the fear of God.

Lord, help us to give each of these areas to You, that we would no longer live according to the will of man, but according to the will and standard of God. When we give these areas to You, help us to leave these areas of sin at the foot of the cross-to never take them up again.

For Your glory,
in Jesus's name
Amen.

CHAPTER 6

How Did We Get Here?
Or, Where Are We?

In this chapter, I want to look at some passages that I think will help us to answer the above questions.

The teaching and principles expressed and taught in these passages should help all of us examine our walk with the Lord, not justify or rationalize the areas in which we have strayed. Before going any further, please read God's indictments against the nation of Israel in Malachi.

Notice at the end of Malachi 4:6, what the Lord states will happen to those who reject the message of "Elijah:" "... Lest I come and strike the earth with a curse."

My friends, God is very serious about sin and the consequences of it. To verify this further, look back at Malachi 3:13-15, and see what was happening in the hearts and lives of the people of the land.

I see that the response to the Prophet Jeremiah by the people of the land speaks volume to us today. It seems that the people of this nation have responded in a similar fashion to those who speak the truth of God today.

"Then all the men who knew that their wives had burned incense to other gods, with all the women who stood by, a great multitude, and all the people who dwelt in the land of Egypt, in Pathros," answered Jeremiah, saying: "As for the word that you have spoken to us in the name of the Lord, we will not listen to you! But we will certainly do whatever has gone out of our own mouths!" (Jer. 44:15-16)

Jeremiah was a true Prophet of God, and he spoke the word of God to the people, as the Lord told him. He spoke the truth (See John 17:17), however, the people wanted to establish their own truth and do that which was right in their own eyes (See Jer. 5:30-31; 2 Tim. 4:1-5).

...there is no truth or mercy or knowledge of God in the land. My people are destroyed for lack of knowledge. Because you have rejected knowledge...because you have forgotten the law of your God... The more they increased, the more they sinned against Me... they set their heart on their iniquity... like people, like priest. So I will punish them for their ways. (Hos. 4:1, 6-9)

There are more verses, which can be shared from this text, but the highlights that have been shared here help us to understand the heart of the people of the nation. Each one continued to do what was right in their own eyes and had forgotten the Lord and His Word in all their ways. They sought to establish their own righteousness. (See Prov. 14:12; 16:25).

> They set up kings, but not by Me; They made princes and I did not acknowledge it... (Hos. 8:4)

In Hosea 8–9:1, we can see five basic reasons for God's judgment against the nation:

Hos. 8:4-6 – They were given to idolatry.

Hos. 8:9 – They had turned to other nations, not the Lord.

Hos. 8:11-13 – There was no substance to their worship.

Hos. 8:14 – They had forgotten their Creator.

Hos. 9:1 – They had played the harlot with other nations. This is far worse, as it deals with an expression of prostitution.

From the text of Hosea we need to understand that part of the problem with the nation is that they did not even consider God, or His standard of leadership, when they were putting kings in power. Modern terminology: God was left out when they held their "election." He was nowhere to be found in the process.

Does Hosea 8:4 contradict Romans 13? Certainly not; God established the office, not necessarily the occupant of that office. The bottom line is that nations get the leadership that they deserve. (See Prov. 29:2–by principle).

There is something else that I would like to point out about the expression, "...but not by Me." Could this also mean that the official was put in that position through dishonest means or tactics? Since God is Holy, righteous, and just, then putting someone in that position through deceit of any kind would violate His very nature and character, would it not? So, then that would not be by Him.

God rejected the worship of the nation because the nation largely rejected the standard of worship that God had established as being acceptable to Him.

The nation continued to trust and make alliances with other nations, which were the enemies of God. Those alliances would be based on provisions, protection, and sometimes, out of the fear of the enemy nation. Much like a bullied schoolboy would do to appease a bully so that the bully would leave him alone. These nations were God's enemies. However, God's nation trusted them over the One who was truly over their nation.

How many times did God say to the nation that He would do all of these things for them, if they would trust and obey Him? There are other examples that could be cited here, but you get the idea. Do any of these things sound familiar to anyone?

> Those things you have done, and I kept silent; You thought that I was altogether like you; But I will reprove you, and set them in order before your eyes. (Psa. 50:21)

The nation did not exalt, glorify, or recognize God for who He is, but rather reduced Him to an image made like corruptible man

(See Rom. 1:22-23). Because God did not exercise judgment against their sins (See Psa. 50:16-20) immediately, they saw Him as being tolerant, accepting, and passive, instead of Holy, righteous, just, patient, merciful, and gracious (See Rom. 2:4). This is similar to what we see in this and other nations today.

> You who turn justice to wormwood, and lay righteousness to rest in the earth! They hate the one who rebukes in the gate, And they abhor the one who speaks uprightly. … you afflict the just and take bribes; You divert the poor from justice at the gate. (Amos 5: 7, 10, 12)

Notice what the people reject, and what is lacking in the nation: justice, righteousness, truth, correction. What do the people practice? Afflicting those whom God has declared as just, taking bribes (which includes trading favors), and oppressing the poor.

Now, the people were practicing these things, yet, they anticipated and or wanted "the day of the Lord." Please take a few minutes to read Amos 5:16-27, very carefully. The Lord pronounced a "woe" of condemnation against those who live in unrighteousness, yet wanted the Lord's return (see verses 18-20).

> He who justifies the wicked, and he who
> condemns the just, both of them alike are
> an abomination to the Lord.(Prov. 17:15)

Can you think of any examples of these two practices, or even one of these practices, that haves happened, or is happening now? Are both of these not happening in the churches and the government today on various levels?

Stick with me a little while longer. I know that you have understood what the purpose and point is by now. I think the last two passages used here will help to solidify that which has been stated thus far.

> Then Peter took Him aside and began
> to rebuke Him, saying, "Far be it from

You Lord; this shall not happen to You!"
(Matt. 16:22)

In this context, Jesus asks His disciples about His iden-
tity (vss.13-20). Right after that He testifies to them that
He is getting ready fulfill the purpose for which He came
(See verse 21).

In verse 22, notice something specific. Peter calls Him
"Lord," but tries to tell Him what is right and wrong and
or the right thing to do. Is that not what we do when we
re-write or re-interpret Scripture to suit our own needs or
to accomplish our own purpose? (Luke 6:46) Alternatively,
put another way, "Lord, I know what You wrote, but let me
tell You what You meant."

For all seek their own, not the things which
are of Christ Jesus. (Phil. 2:21)

This verse ties directly into several of the other verses
previously stated, people doing that which is right in their
own eyes and either ignoring Scripture all together, or
twisting it for their own needs or purposes. Justification
and rationalization become key components when this is
the approach to Scripture.

One last thought in closing this chapter: I have been
talking about the practices of the people in the nation and
how those practices lead to, and have led to, God's judgment coming upon the nation, and the people of the nation.

However, I want to take this teaching to a different arena, by asking a couple of questions. I know that this was addressed previously in this writing, but it was very brief. I wanted to address it a bit further here.

What about our "entertainment?" Are any of these Scripture violations in the movies that we watch? What about the music we choose to listen to or share with others? How about the books that we read? How about the games that we play? Would this not also be a violation of God's Word, even though it is happening in our own home and we are not "directly" participating in the act?

Five Scripture reminders:

> Therefore, come out from among them and be separate says the Lord. Do not touch what is unclean, and I will receive you. (2 Cor. 6:17)

(Please read 2 Cor. 6:11-18, to understand the full impact of God's counsel concerning this matter).

> And have no fellowship with the unfruitful works of darkness, but rather expose them. (Eph. 5:11)

(Again, please read the context to receive the fullest impact of God's counsel).

> For God did not call us to uncleanness, but in holiness. (1 Tim. 4:7)

> Adulterers and adulteresses! Do you not know that friendship with the world is enmity with God? Whoever therefore wants to be a friend of the world makes himself an enemy of God. (James 4:4)

(These words are concise, and inspired by God. He tells us that this is a choice–See Joshua 24:15).

> I will set nothing wicked (by God's standard) before my eyes; I hate the works of those who fall away; it shall not cling to me. A perverse heart shall depart from me; I will not know wickedness. (Psa. 101:3-4)

(Also, read 2 Thessalonians 2:3 to further enhance the understanding of "falling away").

Therefore, with these last five Scripture verses, I close out this chapter.

It is my prayer that the Lord has brought a deeper understanding of His Word to our hearts, and conviction to our lives in the areas where we have strayed. I also hope and pray that He is, and will be, glorified through these very unworthy hands.

May He be honored and glorified as we give these areas of our lives over to Him—permanently. Thus, He would be made Lord of all through a full surrender to Him, His will, and the authority of His Word.

CHAPTER 7

We Can Be Very Sure of "The Final Countdown"

I remember hearing someone state a while ago, "I believe that we are being plunged into a time that the Bible speaks more about than any other time in history; including even the time that Jesus walked the streets of Jerusalem, and calmed the Sea of Galilee." (I think that this is a direct quote, but I am not sure. I do not even remember who made this statement. Still, I do believe that this statement is completely valid).

As stated earlier, there is a judgment coming upon this nation, and the entire world. The Bible testifies to this reality in several different places (See Job 19:25-27—a future resurrection; Isa. 26:20-21; 1 Thess. 4:16-18, 5:9; Rev. 3:10). These are only a few of the verses that testify to the reality of a soon-coming judgment. I have already mentioned others throughout this writing. Also, remember, the soon-coming judgment also means the soon return of the King of kings and the Lord of lords.

There have been many prophecies in the Scripture that have been fulfilled with regard to Israel, the nations, Christ (in His first coming), the prophets, the disciples, Christ's followers, the church, etc. God wrote history in advance. What God has testified to has happened, as He said it would. This leaves no doubt as to whom He is, and to the authority of His Word. (See Isa. 41:20). We can also conclude from the evidence that what God said is about to happen will happen, just as He said it would.

This aspect of the Bible (fulfilled prophecy) is what sets the Bible apart from any other writing. It substantiates its authority, further verifies credibility, and establishes the Bible as true (See Ps.119:89; Prov. 30:5-6; John 17:17; 2 Tim. 3:16-17; 1 Pet. 1:22-25).

If you desire to challenge the authenticity of God's Word, as it is written, research the history of the Jewish people and the nation of Israel (i.e. their history and the current events surrounding that nation) and see for yourself if the Bible is not true. Nevertheless, do not approach Scripture with a pre-conceived notion to try to fit your ideas into His word (See Deut. 4:2; Prov. 30:5-6; Rom. 3:1-6; Rev. 22:18-19). God warns against that!

I wrote all of this for a reason. I do not see the United States in Bible prophecy. However, I do see the practices of this nation defined in Isaiah 5. I mentioned this part of Scripture earlier in this writing, pointing out that God uses the "woes" of condemnation against the practices mentioned.

I have my own theories about why the United States is not specifically mentioned. The United States is possibly included in what the Bible calls, "the islands of the sea," (See Isa. 11:11). Another possibility is that the United States will be absorbed into the ten-nation confederacy, which will dominate the world. (Thus being used to link Mexico and Canada to make one "Super State," under a different or new name). Still another possibility, similar to the last, is that the United States will be overtaken by our enemies and no longer be recognized as the nation that it is today. This nation will no longer exist. Any one of these possibilities is not only frightening, but can also become a reality at any moment (See Jer. 5:9-17–example; Amos 5:10-13).

Subsequently, to close this chapter, I would like to look at some other Scripture verses, and ask some other "challenge questions." (I will be giving some extra verses in each of these sections. Please look them up).

> Why is my pain perpetual and my wound incurable. *Which* refuses to be healed? Will you surely be to me like an unreliable stream, as waters that fail? (Jer. 15:18)

I know that this text is a reference to God's Prophet Jeremiah. Has the wound of this nation become incurable? Are we past the point of no return? I fully believe that we are. Based on Jer. 30:12, and Micah 1:9, I see that these are very pertinent questions.

> We then, as workers together with Him
> also plead with you not to receive the grace
> of God in vain. (2 Cor. 6:1)

(This same teaching applies to Exod. 20:7).

I know some will disagree with what I am about to write, but what if the presentation that I am about to share is correct?

Are we not saved by grace through faith (See Eph. 2:8-10)? So, could these texts be a warning about abusing, misusing, or falsely acquiring Christ's name? Or claiming His name without obedience to Him—salvation, but no commitment to Him (See Matt. 7:21-23; Luke 6:46; Rom. 2-3; 1 John 2).

> For has anyone said to God, 'I have borne
> chastening: I will offend no more: Teach
> me what I do not see; If I have done
> iniquity, I will do no more?' Should He
> repay it according to your terms, Just
> because you disavow it? You choose, and
> not I; Therefore speak what you know.
> (Job 34:31-33)

I believe the challenge of these verses is straightforward. Has anyone genuinely responded to God's chastening in repentance? Are we crying out to God to teach us to see as He does (See Psa. 139:23-24)? Is this not what God is saying to us now? You must choose (See Josh. 24:15; I Kings 18:21).

> "Behold, the days are coming," says the Lord God, "that I will send a famine on the land. Not a famine of bread, Nor a thirst for water, but of hearing the words of the Lord." (Amos 8:11)

This is God's response to a nation that chooses to continue in its rebellion against Him. Also read (Jer. 5:30-31; 1 Tim. 4:1-5; 2 Tim. 3:1-9).

I hope and pray that this writing has been profitable, insightful, and helpful. I know that this writing does not, and will not, answer all questions that may arise from these issues. Only the Bible can do that. Which is why we need to start digging into God's Word for all that it is worth, and allow the Holy Spirit to guide us into all truth (See John 16:13). Neither this writing, nor any other extra biblical writing can, or should, replace God's Word as the final authority to our sin problem.

Therefore, for answers to your questions, there is no replacement for God's Word – the Bible. Be diligent in studying His Word (See 2 Tim. 2:15-16); it is worth it. So is He. You will not be disappointed (See Ps. 119:9, 119:162; Jer. 15:16–also Josh. 1:8).

Though none go with me,
Still I will follow.
No turning back.
No turning back.

(I hope that I am wrong, but I do not think that I am. I see our nation, because of our refusal to heed God's Word, is about to "reap the whirlwind"). (See Hos. 8:7).

Please read the scripture listed: Psalms 81:8-16; Proverbs 2; Luke 13:34-35–by principle; 1 Thessalonians 5:20-22; 1 John 4:1-4.

CHAPTER 8

The Conclusion?

I n this closing chapter, I want to do something different. I want to play a game of sorts. I am going to give some quotes to you to see if you can name the one who spoke these words, when, and maybe give some of their background. See how far our nation, as well as the church, have gone away from Christ and His Word.

Before going on to the quotes, I want to give a biblical challenge to everyone who would take the time to read this writing.

> The coming of the lawless one is according to the working of Satan, with all power, signs, and lying wonders, and with all unrighteous deception among those who perish, because they did not receive the love of the truth, that they might be saved. And for this reason God will send them strong delusion, that they should believe the lie, that they all may be condemned

who did not believe the truth but had pleasure in unrighteousness. (2 Thess. 2:9-12)

Why would I start this chapter in this fashion? These quotes and the time of their utterance will give us all a deeper understanding of the direction that this nation is heading. The order of these quotes will be close to their utterance chronologically. Look carefully at the entire quote that is mentioned and see if you can identify the speaker, the position that they held, and or the time when they spoke these words. Some of them may surprise you.

Quote #1 – (Not a full quote – there is much more to it): "... grateful to Almighty God for the blessings of civil and religious liberty, and humbly invoking His guidance..."[4]

Quote #2 – (Not a full quote – there is much more to it): "... grateful to God for our civil, political, and religious liberties, and desiring to secure them to ourselves and perpetuate them to our posterity..."[5]

Quote #3 – "Those who will not be ruled and governed by God, will be ruled by tyrants."[6]

Quote #4 – At the beginning of each session of the court, as the Justices stand before their desks, the crier opens with the invocation:

"God save the United States and this Honorable Court."[7]

(Look at the decision of this court, and read it carefully, if you can access it anymore. This was the case of Vidal vs. Girard's Executors, 43 U.S. 126, 132, Date 1844). There are others just like this one.

Quote #5 – "The existence of the Bible, as a book for the people, is the greatest benefit which the human race has ever experienced. Every attempt to belittle it is a crime against humanity."[8]

Quote #6 - "May we begin to see that all true Americanism begins in being Christian; that it can have no other foundation, as it has no other roots. To Thy glory was this Republic established. For the advancement of the Christian faith did the Founding Fathers give their life's heritage, passed down to us."[9] (Please do yourself a favor and look this up when you finish reading this writing, for the entire quote).

Quote #7 – "We confess, O Lord, that we think too much of ourselves, for ourselves, and about ourselves. If our Lord had thought about Himself, we would not now be bowed in prayer, nor have the liberty in which and for which to pray. If the great men whom we honor for their part in building our Nation had thought about themselves, we would have no free Republic today. Help us to see, O Lord, that "I" is in the middle of sin, and let no man among us think more highly of himself than he ought to think, to the end that we may be used of Thee in Thy service for the good of all mankind. Through Jesus Christ our Lord. Amen."[10]

Quote #8 – "We need a prophet who will have the ear of America and say to her now, "How long will you halt and stand between two opinions? If the Lord (YHWH) be God, follow Him, but if Baal be God, then follow him; and go to hell!"[11]

Quote #9 – "...Clerk. Once an infidel and libertine a servant of slaves in Africa was by the rich mercy of OUR LORD and SAVIOR JESUS CHRIST preserved, restored, pardoned and appointed to preach the faith he had long labored to destroy."[12]

Quote #10 – "...underneath each of us is a "golden Buddha," a "golden Christ" or "a golden essence," which is our real self."[13]

Quote #11 – "For the Son of God became man so that we might become God."[14]

Quotee #12 – "The Bible says, 'He rules everything and is everywhere and is in everything.'"[15]

Quote #13 – "We no longer feel ourselves to be guests in someone else's home and therefore obligated to make our behavior conform with a set of preexisting cosmic rules. It is our creation now. We make the rules. We establish the parameters of reality. We create the world, and because we do, we no longer feel beholden to outside forces. We no longer have to justify our behavior, for we are now the architects of the universe. We are responsible to nothing outside ourselves, for we are the kingdom, the power, and the glory forever and ever."[16]

Quote #14 – (This is not a direct quote, but all that I could remember from the presentation). "Whatever we once were, we are no longer a Christian nation now."[17]

Quote #15 – "Let me control the textbooks, and I will control the state."[18]

Quote #16 – "If you tell a lie long enough, loud enough, and often enough, the people will believe it."[19]

There are so many more quotes that could be cited here, but these are enough for us to see the constant deterioration of this nation's foundation. You will see that some of these quotes are not just from government officials, but also from some who have "named the name of Christ."

OK. Are you ready for the revealing of the sources of these quotes and statements? Well, hold on, because you may not believe or accept some of them. Just so you know, I am not doing this out of anything but love. Love for Christ, for His Word, for the people to whom He has called me to minister, for those who govern in this nation, and for this nation. When you really love someone, you tell them the truth. No matter how much it hurts, whether they want to hear it or not.

Quote #1 – The Constitution of the State of Pennsylvania. 1776.

Quote #2 – The Constitution of the State of Wyoming, 1890. (Have you looked at the original Constitution for your state? Each state does have one. Additionally, each state recognizes and acknowledges God in this fashion).

Quote #3 – William Penn to Peter the Great, Czar of Russia.

Quote #4 – U.S. Supreme Court – since established.

Quote #5 – Immanuel Kant (1724-1804) – German philosopher – "Critique of Pure Reason" – 1781.

Quote #6 – "Prayer for America" – Peter Marshall appointed Chaplain to the U.S. Senate 1947-1949.

Quote #7 – "Prayer in the Eightieth Congress – 2nd session – Thursday, Feb. 5, 1948 – Peter Marshall.

Quote #8 – Sermon – "Trial By Fire" – from I Kings 18:21 – March 1944 – St. Charles Pres. Church, New Orleans,

Louisiana. (Peter Marshall) (I have one very important question: Do you think that Peter Marshall would be appointed chaplain or even pray this type of prayer in Congress today?)

Quote #9 –on the tombstone of John Newton – 1725-1807 – the author of "Amazing Grace." (Do we have this type of repentant heart today, even in this church? Could we pen words like this and mean them?)

Quote #10 – Jack Canfield – Chicken Soup for the Soul 101 Stories to Open the Heart and Rekindle the Spirit, page 69. (Is this not an expression of idolatry by God's standard?)

Quote #11 - #460 – Catechism of the Catholic Church, pg. 229

Quote #12 – Rick Warren – Purpose Driven Life – "What on Earth Am I Here For?" – pg. 88

Quote #13 – Jeremy Rifkin – "Algeny" – pg. 244

Quote #14 – Barak Obama – From several speeches before the multitudes after becoming President of the United States.

Quote #15 and 16 – Adolf Hitler.

These are not accusations friends, these are quotes that these people either have spoken directly, or have written for all to see or hear.

Did you notice how far we have digressed? From the recognition of and reverence for God, to man replacing God and or claiming to be God. It did not take long for this to happen. God's judgment of this nation has been silent for about 300 years—we are past due. I heard this statement before and I think that it is appropriate to use it here: "If God does not judge America soon, He is going to have to apologize to Sodom and Gomorrah." (See Exod. 23:22). Notice the condition and God's response; no compromise.

As we read 2 Chronicles 36:15-16, we see from Scripture that God sends warnings to the people who He loves, by messengers that He has raised up for the time. What is critical is the response of the people to God's message. (What happened to Nineveh when Jonah preached to them? What about after that?)

> Psalms 33:12 – According to this verse, how is a nation blessed?

> Psalms 78:31ff. – Notice when they sought Him, but also notice what their response to God's judgment was.

> Ezekiel 28:2, 7 – Aren't the people of the nation of the context of the same mindset

with the people of this nation? What was God's response to them? (See verse 7).

Amos 8:11 – Are we also not in this type of spiritual famine in this land today? (If you do not think so, please refer back to the quotes that were mentioned above).

Zechariah 1:4-6, 7:7, 12 – The people that are described in these verses have the same heart condition that is exhibited in the nation. Just look at how people react to the name of Jesus. How about how true Christians are being treated in this nation? How about the laws being passed? Hate crimes laws against those who tell the truth from God's Word, etc.

Matthew 26:39 – Are we really praying the way Jesus did in the garden that day? Are we praying for God's will, not our own?

Ephesians 4:11-14 – Are we established in the fullness of Christ, or are we still children tossed back and forth by every wind of doctrine?

Philippians 3:8 – Do we count all things lost for the excellence of the knowledge of Christ Jesus our Lord? Do we count all things as rubbish to gain Christ?

Colossians 1:21-23 – Are we continuing in the faith? Are we really grounded and steadfast, or are we moved away from the gospel?

Colossians 2:8-9 – Have we heeded this warning?

Jude 3 – Are the Christians contending earnestly for the faith in every place?

I think that I have shared enough Scripture for now, if there is such a thing as enough Scripture. I know that I have not shared much of what some might call "good news" verses. Nevertheless, if you look at the texts of some of the verses that the Lord led me to share, you will see God's response to the people when they did obey.

This nation cannot expect the blessing of God when it calls evil good, re-labels or re-defines sin, excuses injustice, perverts righteousness, and or trashes His Word and His name, all in the name of religious or political "freedom." It is God who granted those freedoms, and I have never read anywhere in His Word where He gave us the authority or "freedom" to violate Him or His Word in any way or for any reason.

I thank you for taking the time to read this writing. I pray that it was helpful and maybe answered some questions that you might have had. Maybe it challenged you to ask some questions that would make us more like the sons of Issachar—to be discerners of the times in which we live.

Endnotes

1   *Oxford's Old English Dictionary* from CD (Logos Bible Software, Scholar's Library, Platinum Edition, version 4.5, Copyright 2012), Page 16.

2   *Vine's Complete Expository Dictionary of Old and New Testament Words* (Nashville Tennessee: Thomas Nelson Publishers, Inc., 1985) page 587.

3   *Vine's Complete Expository Dictionary of Old and New Testament Words*, page 253.

4   Robert L. Maddex, *State Constitutions of The United States*, (N. W. Washington, D.C.: Congressional Quarterly, Inc. 1998).

5   Maddex, *State Constitutions of The United States.*

6   William J. Federer, *America's God and Country, Encyclopedia of Quotes* (St. Louis, MO: Amerisearch, Inc., 2003).

7   Federer, *America's God and Country, Encyclopedia of Quotes.*

8   William J. Federer, *America's God and Country, Encyclopedia of Quotes* (St. Louis, MO: Amerisearch, Inc., 1998).

9 Dr. Peter Marshall, *The Wartime Sermons of Dr. Peter Marshall* (Dallas, Texas: Clarion Call Marketing, Inc., 2005).

10 Marshall, *The Wartime Sermons of Dr. Peter Marshall.*

11 Marshall, *The Wartime Sermons of Dr. Peter Marshall.*

12 "Quote on Tombstone of John Newton" Wikipedia, accessed July 2021, wikipedia.org>wiki>John_Newton.

13 Caryl Matrisciana and Roger Oakland, *The Evolution Conspiracy*, Updated Edition (Eureka, Montana: Lighthouse Trails Publishing, 2016).

14 Matrisciana and Oakland, *The Evolution Conspiracy*, Updated Edition.

15 Matrisciana and Oakland, *The Evolution Conspiracy*, Updated Edition.

16 Matrisciana and Oakland, *The Evolution Conspiracy*, Updated Edition.

17 As remembered by Bruce Zavatsky from several speeches heard on radio and internet during the term of President Obama

18 *The Dangers of Evolution,* by Dr. Kent Hovind, (2002; Pensacola, FL: Creation Science Evangelism, 2002, DVD.

19 Hovind, *The Dangers of Evolution.*

CPSIA information can be obtained
at www.ICGtesting.com
Printed in the USA
LVHW081700180422
716540LV00014B/410

9 781662 846335